H.F.F.

The 10-Minute Monthly Plan to Budget, Save, and Achieve Financial Freedom

A Simple, Stress-Free System to Saving, Paying Bills & Building Wealth in Just Two Years

First published by Independently published 2024

Copyright © 2024 by H.F.F.

All rights reserved. No part of this publication may be reproduced, stored or transmitted in any form or by any means, electronic, mechanical, photocopying, recording, scanning, or otherwise without written permission from the publisher. It is illegal to copy this book, post it to a website, or distribute it by any other means without permission.

First edition

ISBN: 9798302424822

This book was professionally typeset on Reedsy. Find out more at reedsy.com

Contents

Introduction	1
Stop Overthinking Your Money—Here's a Plan That Actually Works	1
The Problem: Modern Life is a Financial Dumpster Fire	2
Why You're Here (and Why I Wrote This Book)	2
1 The Key to Overcoming Common Financial Problems	5
The Financial Struggles of Our Time	5
How Habits Work	6
Building Financial Discipline	7
2 Assessing Your Financial Goals and Mindset	8
Knowing Your Financial Objectives	8
Developing a 'Savings' Attitude	9
Establishing Specific Goals	10
Step 1: Identify Your Goals	11
3 2 Minutes to Categorize and Understand Your Bills	15
1: Identifying Fixed, Variable, and Discretionary Expenses	15
2: Analyze Your Spending	17
3: Find savings opportunities:	17
Action Plan	19
4 2 Minutes to Automate and Overpay	21

The Power of Automation	21
The Overpayment Strategy	23
Avoiding Debt Traps	25
5 3 Minutes to "Roll Over" Unused Funds	28
What Rolling Over Means	29
Tracking Surplus with a Simple System	30
Making It a Habit	32
6 3 Minutes to Track and Reassess Progress	34
The Importance of Regular Reviews	35
Monthly Financial Check-In	37
Adjusting Your Plan for Bigger Wins	38
Why This Matters	40
7 Your 10-Minute Path to Financial Freedom	42
The Simplicity of Small Steps	42
Final Thoughts: Small Wins, Big Changes	43
Your Journey Starts Now	43

Introduction

Stop Overthinking Your Money—Here's a Plan That Actually Works

Let's be honest: managing money sucks. It's stressful, time-consuming, and no matter how many budgeting apps or spreadsheets you try, the whole process feels like an endless, soul-draining chore. Yet, somehow, society expects you to juggle rising bills, inflation, debt, and the looming threat of your friends sending Venmo requests labeled "for dinner" (when they conveniently forgot you didn't eat that night). Sound familiar? Welcome to the club.

But here's the kicker: managing money *doesn't have to suck.*

This book is about a simple, ridiculously effective solution I like to call *The 10-Minute Monthly Plan to Budget, Save, and Achieve Financial Freedom.* It's a system designed for people like you—people who are tired of the constant stress of bill payments and the guilt that comes with not saving "enough." You don't need a degree in finance, a six-figure income, or a crystal ball to make this work. All you need is 10 minutes a month and a willingness to embrace a strategy that's so simple you'll wonder why nobody taught you this in high school.

The Problem: Modern Life is a Financial Dumpster Fire

Let's talk about why this book matters.

We live in a world that's designed to bleed us dry. Prices rise faster than your last attempt to stick to a New Year's resolution, debt feels like it's written into adulthood's fine print, and financial advice online swings between "stop buying coffee" and "invest in real estate." Oh, great, thanks. Let me just buy a duplex with the $3.47 I saved by skipping Starbucks.

Add to that the sheer amount of financial noise out there. Everyone's telling you what to do, but none of it feels realistic. Because let's face it: you're busy. You have work, family, social obligations, and maybe even a Netflix queue that's longer than the list of your financial anxieties. Who has time to map out complicated budgets or analyze investment portfolios for hours every week? Not you, and not the people who will benefit from this strategy.

That's where this book comes in.

Why You're Here (and Why I Wrote This Book)

Chances are, you're reading this because you want something different. Maybe you're tired of living paycheck to paycheck.

INTRODUCTION

Maybe you've tried saving before, but life—car repairs, surprise medical bills, or an "emergency" vacation—got in the way. Or maybe, deep down, you feel like you've failed at this whole "money thing" and are hoping this book has the magic answer. Spoiler alert: it does.

You see, I wrote this book because I've been where you are. I know what it feels like to lie awake at night wondering if your checking account will survive the week. I know the shame of not having a plan and the frustration of every attempt to "fix" things ending in failure. But I also know this: you can turn it around, and it doesn't have to take all your time, energy, or sanity to do it.

The 10-Minute Monthly Plan is about focusing on what *actually works*—a simple, repeatable system that gives you control over your bills, helps you build savings (without feeling like you're sacrificing your happiness), and keeps you on track toward financial freedom. It's not flashy, and it's not about cutting corners. It's about being smart, intentional, and consistent.

By the end of this book, you'll have a system so effective that you'll wonder how you ever lived without it. But more importantly, you'll feel confident in your ability to manage your money, free from the guilt, stress, and overwhelm that's been holding you back.

Here's the hard truth though: this strategy is only as good as your commitment to it. If you're looking for a one-time magic fix, you might as well close this book now and save yourself the disappointment. The only way this works is if you show up—every month, no excuses—for the next two years. Think of it like brushing your teeth. You wouldn't skip that for months on end (at least, I hope not), so why would you skip taking care of your financial health? This plan thrives on consistency, not perfection. It's not about how much money you start with or how perfectly you follow every step—it's about showing up, month after month, and letting those small, intentional actions snowball into life-changing results. So, if you're ready to commit, let's get to work. If not, I'll see you in a couple of years when you're still Googling "how to save money fast.

So, take a deep breath. You're about to learn the one strategy that will make all the difference. And yes, it'll only take you 10 minutes a month. Let's get started.

1

The Key to Overcoming Common Financial Problems

Let's talk about the financial elephant in the room: life is expensive. Like, absurdly expensive. Between student loans, credit card debt, and the occasional $300 "emergency" trip to Target that somehow only got you two candles and a throw blanket, it's no wonder so many people are drowning financially. And the worst part? It feels never-ending.

The Financial Struggles of Our Time

Here's the deal: consumer debt is at an all-time high, student loans are basically modern-day indentured servitude, and the average person's financial literacy stops somewhere around "Don't spend all your money on pizza." Combine that with inflation, rising living costs, and the fact that no one seems to know what the heck a 401(k) actually does, and it's clear: we're all just winging it.

But wait, it gets worse. Mismanaging bills—that is, paying them late, forgetting them altogether, or just pretending they don't exist—adds fuel to the financial dumpster fire. Late fees pile up, interest rates climb, and the stress of it all practically begs you to spend $50 on "self-care" just to feel better. It's a vicious cycle, and breaking out of it feels about as likely as winning the lottery. Spoiler alert: you're not winning the lottery.

Oh, and let's not forget impulsive spending. You tell yourself, "It's just $5," but $5 becomes $50, then $500, and suddenly your Amazon cart has more red flags than your last relationship. The truth is, most of us are flying blind, making decisions in the moment without a clear plan—or any plan, really—and hoping for the best.

How Habits Work

Here's the good news: you're not doomed. The bad news? You're going to have to change your habits.

Let's break it down: every habit—good or bad—follows the same basic pattern: cue, routine, reward. The cue is the trigger (like getting a bill in your inbox). The routine is the action (you either pay it, procrastinate, or panic). And the reward? That depends. If you paid the bill, the reward is peace of mind. If you procrastinate, the reward is temporary relief, but future-you gets stuck with the stress bomb.

The trick to building better habits isn't to overhaul your life overnight. That's a recipe for burnout. Instead, focus on small, sustainable changes that feel so easy you can't mess them up. Like this book's 10-minute-a-month strategy. It's simple, repeatable, and designed to help you build the muscle memory of responsible financial habits.

Think of it like going to the gym—except instead of squats and deadlifts, you're lifting your financial game. And let's be real, squats don't pay the bills.

Building Financial Discipline

If you're looking for a flashy, get-rich-quick scheme, this isn't it. Financial discipline isn't sexy, but it's effective. It's the quiet, unglamorous practice of showing up every month, managing your bills, tracking your expenses, and putting money aside—even when you don't feel like it.

Consistency is the magic sauce here. Think of your financial health like a garden. If you don't water it regularly (aka manage your bills and savings), weeds will take over (aka debt and stress). But if you tend to it every month, even for just 10 minutes, you'll start to see things grow—slowly at first, and then suddenly, as everything starts to compound.

And here's the reframe: paying your bills isn't just about avoiding late fees or debt collectors. It's about creating freedom. Every time you pay a bill on time, every time you track where your money goes, you're taking a step closer to a future where money doesn't control you. It's not just a chore; it's a declaration.

So, are you ready to ditch the excuses and start building financial habits that actually work? Good. Because your future self is counting on you.

2

Assessing Your Financial Goals and Mindset

Here's the thing about money: if you don't tell it where to go, it'll disappear faster than a box of donuts in a break room. The key to not being broke isn't just earning more—it's knowing what you actually want your money to *do* for you. Because money isn't just about stuff; it's about freedom, security, and, let's be honest, fewer awkward moments when splitting the check. So, let's figure out where you're headed.

Knowing Your Financial Objectives

Think of your financial goals like a GPS for your money. If you don't know the destination, you're just driving around in circles, burning gas, and wondering why you're not getting anywhere. That's why we're starting with the basics: what do you actually want?

Let's break this down into two categories:

1. **Short-term goals**: These are the "I need to deal with this now" objectives. Think debt repayment, building an emergency fund, or finally paying back your friend for that concert ticket they fronted you last year.
2. **Long-term goals**: These are your big-picture dreams. Buying a house, retiring early, or saving up for the kind of vacation where you don't have to share a room with six people to afford it.

Here's a quick exercise: write down the three things that keep you up at night when you think about money. Congratulations, those are your short-term goals. Now, write down the three things that make you smile when you think about money. Those are your long-term goals.

Developing a 'Savings' Attitude

Here's a harsh truth: most of us suck at saving because we're stuck in a scarcity mindset. It's that little voice in your head that says, *"I'll never have enough,"* or *"What's the point of saving when life is just going to throw another curveball?"*

Let's change that.

The first step is flipping the script from scarcity to abundance. Instead of thinking, *"I can't afford this,"* start asking, *"How can I make this work?"* Saving isn't about deprivation—it's about giving future-you a high-five for being so damn responsible.

And guess what? The psychological benefits of financial discipline are real. When you take control of your money, you feel less stressed, more confident, and—dare I say—happier. Saving isn't just about the money; it's about proving to yourself that you've got this.

Establishing Specific Goals

Let's talk about SMART goals. No, not "study harder" smart—this kind:

- **Specific**: What exactly do you want? No vague nonsense like "save more money." How much, and by when?
- **Measurable**: Can you track your progress? If not, it's just wishful thinking.
- **Achievable**: Don't set yourself up for failure. Saving $10K in six months is great… unless your income is $2K a month.
- **Relevant**: Does this goal align with what actually matters to you? If you don't care about home ownership, don't put "save for a down payment" on your list.
- **Time-bound**: Deadlines make things real. Commit to a timeline, and don't leave it open-ended like your "someday" fitness plan.

Here's a practical worksheet to make this easy:

ASSESSING YOUR FINANCIAL GOALS AND MINDSET

Step 1: Identify Your Goals

This worksheet is designed to help you clarify your financial objectives and set actionable, achievable goals. Print it out or recreate it in a notebook to start planning.

Short-term goals (Goals you want to achieve within 1 year)	Mid-term goals (Goals for the next 2-5 years)	Long-term goals (Goals for 5+ years from now)
Example: Pay off $1,000 in credit card debt.	Example: Save $10,000 for a car.	Example: Save $50,000 for a home down payment.
My Goal:	My Goal:	My Goal:

Step 2: Prioritize Your Goals

Rank your goals in order of importance:

1.
2.
3.
4.
5.

Step 3: Make Your Goals SMART

For each goal, use the table below to turn it into a SMART goal:

Goal Description	Specific	Measurable	Achievable	Relevant	Time Bound
Example: Emergency Fund	$5,000	Yes	Yes	Yes	12 Months

Step 4: Break Down Your Goals

Use this section to break your goals into smaller, manageable monthly targets.

Goal Description	Total Goal Amount	Monthly Target	Start Date	End Date
Example: Emergency Fund	$5,000	$417	Jan 2024	Dec 2024

Step 5: Plan for Adjustments

Sometimes life throws a curveball. List one or two ways you'll adjust your spending if something unexpected happens:

Example: Skip takeout for two weeks to cover a sudden car repair.

Adjustment 1: _____
_____
_____.

Adjustment 2: _____
_____
_____.

Adjustment 3: _____
_____
_____.

Adjustment 4: _____
_____
_____.

Step 6: Visualize Success

Write a quick description of how achieving these goals will improve your life.

Example: *"By saving $10,000 in 2 years, I'll feel secure knowing I can handle any emergencies and take my dream vacation guilt-free."*

My Vision: _____

THE 10-MINUTE MONTHLY PLAN TO BUDGET, SAVE, AND ACHIEVE FINANCIAL FREEDOM

_____
_____
_____
_____.

These worksheets keep your goals front and center and help you track progress. Keep them somewhere visible—on your desk, fridge, or wherever you'll see it often—and commit to reviewing it monthly.

Remember, small wins build momentum. It's not about saving thousands overnight; it's about taking one consistent step at a time.

Now that you've set your goals and started thinking like a financial ninja, we're ready to dive into the meat of the plan. Because let's be honest, dreaming about financial freedom is fun, but achieving it? That's where the real magic happens.

3

2 Minutes to Categorize and Understand Your Bills

Let's be real—most of us have no idea where our money goes. It's like some sneaky financial black hole that swallows $20 here, $50 there, and then laughs in your face when you check your bank account. But here's the thing: the first step to fixing your finances is knowing exactly where your money is going. Welcome to the glorious (and slightly painful) process of categorizing your bills.

1: Identifying Fixed, Variable, and Discretionary Expenses

Think of your expenses as a dysfunctional family. You've got:

1. **Fixed Expenses:** The reliable ones that never change—rent, car payments, insurance. These are like your boring uncle who wears the same sweater to every holiday dinner.
2. **Variable Expenses:** These are unpredictable but

necessary—utilities, groceries, gas. They're the cool cousin who's always traveling and can't commit to anything.

3. **Discretionary Expenses:** These are the wild cards—streaming subscriptions, dining out, impulse purchases. Basically, the drama queen of the group who needs constant attention.

Now, use this next worksheet and jot down every expense you can think of. Print it out or recreate it to track your financial "dysfunctional family." Don't worry about perfection—we're aiming for awareness, not financial sainthood.

Expense Name	Monthly Cost	Fixed Expense	Variable Expense	Discretionary Expense
rent	$1,500	✓		
Total				

2: Analyze Your Spending

Let's find out the total for each category:

- Fixed Expenses: $_____
- Variable Expenses: $_____
- Discretionary Expenses: $_____

This step is about gaining clarity. Most people feel like their money "disappears" every month, but when you analyze spending, you're forcing yourself to face the reality of where your money is going. Break your expenses into categories (Fixed, Variable, Discretionary) and total them up.

Ask yourself:

What surprises me? Did you realize you spend $100 a month on streaming subscriptions or $300 on dining out? Identifying these is eye-opening.

Are my spending habits aligned with my priorities? If saving for an emergency fund or paying off debt is a goal, but most of your money is going to non-essentials, it's time for a shift.

3: Find savings opportunities:

Here's where the magic happens—you spot areas where you can save without drastically changing your lifestyle. Look at each category critically:

1. **Fixed Expenses:**

- **Negotiate bills:** Many companies (cable, internet, phone) will reduce rates if you call and ask for discounts.
- **Review insurance policies:** Shop around for better deals or bundles.
- **Cancel unused services:** Gym memberships or magazine subscriptions you're not using are money down the drain.

1. **Variable Expenses:**

- **Meal planning:** Reduce grocery costs by planning meals, using a shopping list, and avoiding impulse buys.
- **Energy-saving hacks:** Lower utility bills with small changes like using energy-efficient bulbs or running appliances during off-peak hours.

1. **Discretionary Expenses:**

- **Cut redundant subscriptions:** Do you need three streaming services? Pick one or two.
- **Budget for treats:** Allocate a specific amount for entertainment and stick to it.
- **DIY options:** Brew coffee at home instead of buying it every morning; host movie nights instead of going out.

So, recap.
Ask yourself:

- Are there any unnecessary Fixed Expenses? (e.g., extra insurance add-ons)

_____
_____.

- Can you trim Variable Expenses? (e.g., meal planning to cut grocery costs)

_____
_____.

- Are Discretionary Expenses worth it? (e.g., canceling unused subscriptions)

_____
_____.

Action Plan

Once you've analyzed your spending and found savings opportunities, you need a concrete plan to implement changes. Start with one or two actionable steps to avoid feeling overwhelmed.
Example Plan:

1. **Cancel subscriptions:** I will cancel [specific subscription] by [specific date], saving $X/month.
2. **Set grocery limits:** I will budget $200/month for groceries by meal planning weekly.
3. **Track progress:** I will revisit my spending every two weeks to ensure I'm on track.

Write down one/two expense you'll cut or reduce this month:

- I will reduce/cancel _____, saving $_____ per month.
- I will reduce/cancel _____, saving $_____ per month.

Keep this worksheet handy and review it monthly. Tracking your expenses regularly is the first step to financial clarity and control! Remember, the goal is consistency, not perfection. Even small changes can lead to big results over time!

From here on we will look at the 10-Minute Monthly strategy and label each chapter to the amount of minutes it will take you each month to get that job done.

4

2 Minutes to Automate and Overpay

Managing your bills shouldn't be a daunting task. In fact, it doesn't have to take up much of your time at all. With the right strategies in place, bill payment can become a seamless, automatic process that works for you, not against you.

The magic happens when you harness the power of automation and take a proactive approach to overpaying, helping you prevent debt while building a buffer that can take the pressure off during unexpected financial hiccups. In this chapter, we'll dive into how automation and overpayment can simplify your life and set you up for long-term financial success.

The Power of Automation

You know what's fun? NOT worrying about whether your internet bill got paid on time. That's where automation swoops in to save the day. When you automate your bill payments, you're essentially putting your financial life on cruise control, giving you the peace of mind that everything is getting taken care of on time. Gone are the days of scrambling to pay your bills before the due date, or worse, forgetting entirely.

Setting up automated bill payments is like hiring a personal assistant—only this one doesn't expect coffee breaks or a year-end bonus. You can set it up once, and it'll run like a well-oiled machine, making sure your bills are paid on time, every time. Just a few minutes of setting up, and you can avoid the stress of tracking every bill manually, especially as your financial life gets busier.

Here's how it works:

- **Eliminate Late Fees:** Automation ensures that your bills are paid on time, every time. No more frantic calls to customer service explaining why you "totally meant" to pay the electric bill.

- **Stress-Free Scheduling:** Use your bank's app or a third-party tool to automate recurring expenses like rent, utilities, and subscriptions. Most platforms allow you to choose the day payments are made, so you can align them with your paycheck.

Pro Tip: Set a calendar reminder to review your automated payments once a quarter. Automation is awesome, but it doesn't mean you should go on autopilot forever.

The Overpayment Strategy

Now, let's take your bill-paying game up a notch. If automation is the engine, overpayment is the turbo boost. Paying a little extra on fixed expenses now can save you from financial headaches later. And here's where it gets even better: overpayments aren't just sitting in a black hole. They're being applied toward your future bills, so you'll owe less in the coming months. This creates a cycle of financial freedom, where your bills gradually get smaller, and your savings continue to grow.

Here's how overpaying works:

- **Build a Cushion:** For bills like utilities or rent, overpaying by even $10-$20 a month creates a financial buffer. One bad month (hello, surprise car repairs) won't derail you because you've already prepaid part of your bills.

- **Compound Savings:** The overpaid amount doesn't just sit there—it reduces what you owe in the following months. That's cash you can redirect toward savings or debt repayment.

Fill out this worksheet to get a better understanding:

THE 10-MINUTE MONTHLY PLAN TO BUDGET, SAVE, AND ACHIEVE FINANCIAL FREEDOM

Category	Payment	Overpay/Month	Total/Year	Payoff
Utilities (Electric, Gas, Water)	$ _____	$10-$20	$ _____	Redirect overpayment to savings or debt
Rent or Mortgage	$ _____	$10-$20	$ _____	Can use overpayment for emergencies or savings
Phone/Internet Bill	$ _____		$ _____	Use savings toward a long-term goal (retirement, debt repayment)
Insurance (Health, Car, Home)	$ _____		$ _____	
Credit Card/Loan Payments	$ _____		$ _____	

Quick Math Magic: If you overpay $20/month on your electricity bill, that's $240/year. Add a couple more bills, and you're sitting on a tidy chunk of change by year's end.

Overpaying on your bills is actually a powerful strategy to give yourself a financial cushion and reduce your upcoming expenses - building a buffer that gives you flexibility in the future.

Avoiding Debt Traps

Debt traps are like your sneaky ex that creeps up on you when you least expect it. One missed payment here, an unplanned expense there, and suddenly, you're in over your head. But with automation and overpayment in place, you're taking steps to avoid this mess before it even begins. That buffer you created with overpayments in your accounts—created a financial cushion to fall back on in case of a medical emergency or a sudden car repair. It's your safety net. Rather than relying on credit cards or loans to get by, you're using the money you've already overpaid to cover unexpected costs. The key here is using your extra payments wisely. Instead of letting your extra money disappear into spontaneous spending or another coffee run, use it to create more breathing room in your finances.

Here's how this strategy helps you avoid debt traps:

- **Buffer Against Emergencies:** Life happens. Unexpected expenses, like car repairs or medical bills, will show up when you least expect them. But if you've been overpaying on your bills and automating your payments, you're already a few steps ahead. The overpaid amounts can cover you in lean months, preventing you from relying on credit cards or loans.

- **Prevent Interest Overload:** If you're in a cycle of debt (hello, credit card bills), overpaying on your fixed bills can free up cash that you'd otherwise have to dedicate to interest payments. Think of this as your "interest-free zone" where you use the extra balance to prevent yourself from sinking further.

- **Financial Cushion for Flexibility:** You never know when you'll face a tight month, and those unpredictable situations often lead to impulsive, unhealthy financial decisions. Having a buffer gives you the flexibility to be financially smart, instead of feeling cornered and having to make choices you regret later.

Pro Tip: If you do find yourself in a pinch, don't just pay the minimum on debt. Use the overpaid funds from your bills to throw a little extra toward your credit card balance. It's like slashing your way out of a jungle with a machete—slow, but effective.

This proactive approach gives you the financial flexibility to handle life's surprises without falling into debt traps. The goal here isn't to be perfect; it's to make sure you have a safety net that keeps you grounded, no matter what comes your way.

By the time you hit that two-year mark, these little overpayments will not only help you manage your regular expenses but will also give you a solid foundation for handling the unpredictable. So while you're paying those bills, you're also building a financial fortress that stands tall against any debt traps that might try to knock you down. Because this proactive strategy has already paved the way for smoother sailing. And, trust me, you'll be glad you set up this structure now, rather than scrambling later when that "emergency" expense pops up.

5

3 Minutes to "Roll Over" Unused Funds

So, here's the deal: you've paid your bills, stuck to your budget, and—lo and behold—there's money left over. It's like finding cash in your coat pocket when you haven't worn that jacket in months. That's right. The mythical leftover funds that are always a good surprise. But don't get too excited yet. The million-dollar question is, what do you do with it? Do you celebrate with a spontaneous shopping spree, or do you actually *use* that extra cash to move closer to your financial goals? This chapter is all about the latter—taking those extra funds and redirecting them into places that can help you build real financial security. This is the golden opportunity to build real financial momentum. Rolling over unused funds is a small step with a huge payoff, and it's a habit that's easier to develop than you might think.

What Rolling Over Means

Now, when I say "rolling over," I'm not talking about rolling over in bed after hitting the snooze button one too many times. I'm talking about taking the extra money you've saved from not blowing your entire paycheck on fast food, coffee, or that impulse online shopping spree and using it wisely. In the world of finance, rolling over is the magic trick that turns extra cash into something more useful. It means taking the money you didn't spend and moving it into high-impact areas like savings, investments, or debt reduction. You know how you always hear about paying yourself first? Well, rolling over is like paying yourself extra. It's like getting a bonus from your frugal self.

Here's the kicker: you're not just going to leave that leftover cash in your checking account where it'll *disappear* by next month's paycheck. You're putting it somewhere it can actually *work for you*. Why does it matter? Well, it's because money left in your checking account has a funny way of disappearing, as we all know too well. It gets absorbed into those impulse purchases or used as a cushion for the next month's bills. But by intentionally rolling it over into savings or other financial goals, you're actually building your future with something that didn't even require extra effort. It's like planting seeds for financial freedom without even realizing you're doing it. You just need to be intentional about it.

Tracking Surplus with a Simple System

So now that we've established what rolling over is, let's talk about how to actually do it. It's easy to have good intentions, but without a simple system for tracking your surplus funds, you'll likely forget about it by next payday. That's where a simple tracking system comes in. It helps you track what's left over after each month's expenses. And, no, you don't need to be an accountant to do this. This doesn't need to be complicated—just a basic log where you jot down what's leftover each month and decide where it's going.

Here's how it works:

Create a "Leftover Funds" Log: Here's a spreadsheet where at the end of each month, you can jot down how much extra cash you have after all bills and expenses are paid.

Month	Total Income	Total Expenses	Bills Paid	Extra Funds Leftover
	$	$	$	$
	$	$	$	$
	$	$	$	$
	$	$	$	$
	$	$	$	$
	$	$	$	$
	$	$	$	$
	$	$	$	$
	$	$	$	$
	$	$	$	$
	$	$	$	$
	$	$	$	$

Categorize the Funds: Decide what you're going to do with that money. Is it going toward your emergency fund? Is it time to invest in a little side hustle? Or maybe you'll add it to your debt repayment fund?

Set a Consistent Rollover Goal: Each month, aim to roll over a specific percentage of the leftover funds. For example, if you have $100 leftover, roll over $50 and spend the rest guilt-free on something enjoyable, like a night out or a new book (but don't go crazy, okay?).

Pro Tip: If you don't want to track this by hand, set up an automatic transfer from your checking account to your savings or investment account every time a certain balance is reached. Let the system work for you. Remember, financial freedom isn't about finding ways to keep every penny. It's about being strategic with the pennies you *do* keep.

Making It a Habit

Okay, so you've tracked your surplus and you know where it's going. But how do you ensure that this doesn't just become a one-off activity? That's where the power of habit comes in. Building a new habit takes time, but it's a lot easier when you keep it simple and don't overwhelm yourself. With rolling over unused funds, the goal isn't perfection—it's consistency. The more you do it, the more ingrained it will become in your monthly financial routine..

But can YOU make it a habit? Absolutely. And here's how:

- **Consistency Is Key:** The real power of rolling over unused funds comes from doing it every month. Sure, you might have some months where there's not much leftover. That's okay! The goal is consistency, not perfection. Just like brushing your teeth every day, you want rolling over to be a non-negotiable part of your routine.

- **Start Small:** Don't expect to roll over $1,000 in your first month. Start with what you can. If it's $20, then so be it. The point is to start making that habit a part of your life.

- **Reward Yourself**: After a few months of rolling over and building up your savings, celebrate your progress. Do something small, like taking yourself out to dinner (but don't blow your savings on that one). Recognize your efforts and stay motivated.

Bonus Tip: If you can afford it, try using the "round-up" method. Some apps or banks let you round up your purchases to the nearest dollar and automatically transfer the extra cents into your savings. You'd be surprised how quickly that small change adds up.

Remember, this isn't about using all the money you have left over; it's about putting aside a portion that's going to pay off for you in the long run. And if you're someone who struggles with temptation (hello, impulse buyer), consider automating the process. Set up a system where your leftover funds are automatically moved into a separate account, so you don't have to think about it. Once the habit is ingrained, you won't even have to think twice about rolling over your unused funds. You'll build momentum that works for you without forcing any drastic changes.

So ,the next time you look at your bank account and see those extra dollars, remember: it's not a free pass to spend. It's an opportunity to grow your financial foundation one small step at a time. And as you continue this habit, you'll realize something even more amazing: those small habits compound into big results. In two years, you won't just be surviving—you'll be thriving–your future self will thank you for being smart and disciplined today.

6

3 Minutes to Track and Reassess Progress

Let's be honest, tracking and reassessing might not sound as sexy as "rolling over funds" or automating your bills. But this step? This is where the magic happens. Because what's the point of a strategy if you don't check whether it's working—or worse, keep doing the same thing even when it's not? Imagine trying to get fit without ever stepping on a scale or measuring your progress. You'd be running blind, thinking you're crushing it while those daily donuts undo your treadmill sprints. Tracking your finances is the same—except, thankfully, without sweat.

Reassessing your money strategy every month isn't about judgment; it's about staying in control. A regular review keeps your financial goals aligned with your reality (and also keeps those creepy temptations during sale time under control), so you're not working hard just to stand still.

Let's make tracking as easy as sending a text. With just a few minutes each month, you'll know exactly where you stand and how to adjust for the better. It's the financial version of standing on a scale at the end of the week and saying, "Oh, that's why eating pizza every night wasn't such a good idea." Let's break it down.

The Importance of Regular Reviews

When was the last time you checked if your financial strategy was still working for you? If your answer is somewhere between "what strategy?" and "never," don't worry—you're not alone. Most of us set a plan, stick our heads in the sand, and hope it magically works out. Spoiler alert: it doesn't. And before you know, life happens. Your car breaks down, your boss decides bonuses aren't a thing this year, or you binge-order late-night sushi one too many times.

Money management is like driving—if you're not checking the map occasionally, you might end up in the middle of nowhere wondering how you missed all the exits. Regular reviews are your financial GPS. They help you spot the potholes (like sneaky subscription fees), take detours when life throws traffic your way (hello, surprise medical bills), and keep moving toward your destination.

The beauty of these reviews is their simplicity. You don't need spreadsheets longer than a CVS receipt or hours of number crunching. All it takes is three minutes to check where you are, compare it to where you want to be, and adjust accordingly. Think of it like cleaning out your closet. You reassess every few months, tossing out what no longer works (hello, skinny jeans!) and making room for what does. Your financial strategy deserves the same attention.

A quick monthly review helps you:

- Spot leaks in your budget faster than a plumber fixes a pipe.
- Adjust to life's unpredictability (because adulting is just winging it half the time).
- Feel like the boss of your money, not its underpaid intern.

Grab a pen and paper and start writing which of the following (or your own ideas) align with what we discussed here:

Category	What to Review	Your Notes/Adjustments
Budget Leaks	Review last month's expenses. Did you overspend in any category? What caused the leak?	Example: Spent $50 extra on dining out. Plan to prepare meals next month.
Unexpected Costs	List any surprise expenses (e.g., car repairs, medical bills). Can they be avoided in the future?	Example: $200 on car repair. Start a vehicle maintenance savings fund.
Life Changes	Did your income, expenses, or lifestyle change? (e.g., new job, moving, etc.)	Example: Pay cut this month. Reduce entertainment budget by $30.
Successes	What went well? Where did you stick to the plan or exceed your goals?	Example: Staying under grocery budget by $20. Added extra to savings!
Adjustments Needed	Based on this review, what changes will you make for next month?	Example: Cancel underused subscription, reallocate $15 to emergency fund.
New Goals	Set a micro-goal for next month (e.g., save $50, pay off a credit card balance, etc.).	Example: Save $100 for holiday expenses by cutting out weekend takeout.

These ideas should help your creative juices flow and help you think of similar ways you can save each month/year.

Pro tip: Set a reminder on your phone, or tie it to something you already do monthly—like paying bills or, let's be real, scrolling TikTok.

Monthly Financial Check-In

Okay, let's dive into the *how*. A financial check-in is like a casual chat with your budget: "Hey, how've you been? Still working for me?" The goal isn't to shame yourself for overspending on coffee but to learn from the patterns and make adjustments. Let's get practical. This isn't a soul-crushing audit; it's just you and your budget having a heart-to-heart.

Here's how it works:

1. **Review Last Month's Spending**: Open up your bank app, check your expenses, and get a clear picture of where your money went. Any big surprises? Or did it align with your budget categories? If so, bravo!
2. **Measure Progress**: Look at your goals—did you add to your savings? Did you pay off more debt? How much closer are you to that vacation fund, emergency cushion, or debt-free life? Even small wins count here.
3. **Spot Red Flags**: Is there a category you consistently overspend on? Like overspending on takeout? (It's okay; we've all been there.) But maybe it's the reason your "fun money" turns into "fun month." Recognize it without judgment and plan how to improve.

This isn't rocket science, but it does require honesty. Be brutally truthful with yourself, not in a harsh way but in a "we can do better" way. Remember, every great plan evolves, and yours should too.

Fill out this simple template to log these insights to evaluate your financial health, progress, and areas for improvement. It's quick, painless, and sets you up for smarter choices next month.

Category	Questions to Ask Yourself	Your Answers/Notes
Review Last Month's Spending	Did my spending align with my budget categories? List any surprises or overages.	Example: Overspent by $40 on takeout. No surprises, just bad planning.
Big Wins	What went well? Did I meet or exceed my savings or debt-repayment goals?	Example: Saved an extra $50! Paid $100 extra toward credit card balance.
Goals Progress	How much closer am I to my short-term or long-term financial goals?	Example: Vacation fund grew by $200—halfway there!
Next Month's Micro-Goal	Set a small, achievable goal for next month to keep momentum.	Example: Spend $30 less on eating out and move it to the emergency fund.
Red Flags	Which categories need attention? Where am I consistently overspending?	Example: Streaming services—three subscriptions I barely use.
Changes to Make	What specific adjustments will I implement for next month?	Example: Cancel two subscriptions, allocate $20 saved to groceries budget.

Adjusting Your Plan for Bigger Wins

Now that you know what worked and what didn't, it's time to tweak. Small adjustments can lead to big wins. The best part about tracking your progress? It gives you the power to tweak your strategy for maximum impact. Maybe you realized you've been saving more than expected. Fantastic—redirect that extra toward your emergency fund or debt repayment. Or maybe you noticed that your utilities spiked this month—time to dig into why and see if switching providers or cutting back makes sense.

Small adjustments can lead to big wins over time. Think of it like steering a ship. A slight turn may seem minor in the moment, but over weeks and months, it can change your entire trajectory.

Here's how to adjust:

- **Reallocate Funds**: Shift leftover money into categories that need it most. For eg. If you've been overpaying utilities, and now you're months ahead, redirect that extra to your savings.

- **Set Micro Goals**: If saving for a down payment feels overwhelming, break it into smaller monthly targets. For eg. If you're consistently overspending on "fun money," tighten that category by $20 and challenge yourself to get creative with free activities.

- **Test out new strategies**—maybe cutting back on dining out frees up more cash than you thought. For eg. Found

$50 leftover? Boost your debt repayment or finally start that side hustle savings fund.

Adjusting doesn't mean you failed; it means you're paying attention. Imagine an athlete who never changes their game plan. Spoiler: They'd lose. This is your financial game, and every tweak gets you closer to winning. It's not about being perfect; it's about being proactive. And as you track and adjust month after month, you'll notice something amazing: managing money stops feeling like a chore and starts feeling like empowerment.

Why This Matters

Tracking and reassessing isn't just a checkbox—it's the heartbeat of your financial plan. It keeps you focused, adaptable, and in control. Over time, these three minutes will become second nature, and your progress will speak for itself.

Remember, consistency beats intensity every time. Show up for those three minutes every month, and before you know it, you'll be celebrating milestones you once thought impossible. And when that happens? Give yourself a pat on the back—and maybe treat yourself to a donut, guilt-free.

By tracking and reassessing every month, you're doing two things:

1. You're proving to yourself that you can manage money intentionally.

2. You're setting the stage for consistent wins, no matter what life throws your way.

So grab a coffee, sit down with your budget, and make those 3 minutes count. Because every tweak, every adjustment, and every progress report brings you closer to your version of financial freedom.

7

Your 10-Minute Path to Financial Freedom

The Simplicity of Small Steps

Let's take a moment to reflect on what you've achieved just by reading this book. You've unlocked a practical, no-nonsense approach to managing your finances in just 10 minutes a month. From categorizing your bills and automating payments to rolling over savings and reassessing your progress, you now have a system that doesn't demand spreadsheets the size of Mars or hours you don't have.

The power of this strategy lies in its simplicity. It's not about perfection; it's about progress. It's about consistently showing up for your finances—even for just 10 minutes a month—and letting those small, deliberate steps snowball into life-changing results.

Final Thoughts: Small Wins, Big Changes

Here's the thing: financial freedom isn't reserved for the elite, the spreadsheet-savvy, or the ultra-disciplined. It's achievable for anyone willing to trade chaos for a little consistency. And the beauty of this system? You don't have to overhaul your life overnight. You just need to make one better decision at a time, month after month.

Yes, there will be challenges. There will be months when life throws a nasty surprise at you, and sticking to the plan feels harder than running a marathon uphill. That's okay. What matters is that you keep coming back. Financial progress is like building muscle—it's less about intensity and more about consistency.

Your Journey Starts Now

So here's the deal: this book will only work if *you* work it. Pick a day this month—heck, pick *today*—to start implementing what you've learned. Set up your bill categories, automate those payments, and begin your first monthly check-in. The first step is always the hardest, but it's also the most important.

Once you've started, I'd love to hear about your experience. Did this strategy make a difference in your life? Did you finally feel like the boss of your money instead of its servant? If so, please take a moment to leave a review on Amazon. Not only does it help others discover this book, but it also gives me invaluable feedback to make future resources even better.

The road to financial freedom isn't a sprint; it's a marathon you run one step at a time. You've got the roadmap, the tools, and—most importantly—the determination to make it happen. Now go make those 10 minutes count!

www.ingramcontent.com/pod-product-compliance
Lightning Source LLC
Chambersburg PA
CBHW070941220526
45469CB00007B/2475